Lactose intolerance diet cookbook with over **50** dairy-free breakfast, lunch, dinner and desserts recipes for digestive health and overall wellness

Lillie R. Williams

TABLE OF CONTENTS

INTRODUCTION

A large percentage of people around the world suffer from lactose intolerance, a common digestive ailment. Its hallmark is the body's inability to completely digest the sugar lactose, which is present in milk and other dairy products. This condition arises due to insufficient levels of the enzyme lactase, which is responsible for breaking down lactose into simpler sugars that can be easily absorbed by the body. As a result, individuals with lactose intolerance often experience uncomfortable symptoms such as bloating, gas, diarrhea, and stomach cramps after consuming lactose-containing foods.

Managing lactose intolerance involves making conscious dietary choices to minimize or avoid the consumption of lactose. While complete avoidance of all dairy products may not always be necessary, understanding which foods are high in lactose and adopting strategies to minimize discomfort can greatly improve the quality of life for those with lactose intolerance. Meals play a crucial role in this process, offering an opportunity to create a balanced and enjoyable diet that caters to individual preferences and nutritional needs.

In this discussion, we will explore how meals can be tailored to accommodate lactose intolerance, focusing on alternative food sources, lactase supplements, and meal planning strategies that allow individuals to savor their favorite dishes without compromising their digestive comfort. By making informed choices and selecting appropriate foods, individuals with lactose intolerance can still enjoy delicious and nutritious meals while effectively managing their condition.

BREAKFAST RECIPES

Dairy-Free Overnight Oats

Ingredients:

1 cup rolled oats

1 cup almond milk (or any other lactose-free milk)

1 tablespoon chia seeds

1 tablespoon maple syrup or honey

Fresh fruits (e.g., berries, sliced banana) for topping

Instructions:

Combine oats, almond milk, chia seeds, and maple syrup/honey in a bowl. Stir well, cover, and refrigerate overnight. In the morning, top with fresh fruits before serving.

Avocado Toast

Ingredients:

2 slices of whole-grain bread (check for lactose-free option)

1 ripe avocado

Salt and pepper to taste

Optional toppings: sliced tomatoes, red pepper flakes, or balsamic glaze

Instructions:

Toast the bread. While it's toasting, mash the avocado and season it with salt and pepper. Spread the mashed avocado on the toast and add any desired toppings.

Veggie Omelette

Ingredients:

3 large eggs (or plant-based egg substitute)

1/4 cup diced bell peppers

1/4 cup diced onions

1/4 cup sliced mushrooms

Salt and pepper to taste

Olive oil

Instructions:

In a bowl, whisk the eggs (or egg substitute) and season with salt and pepper. In a non-stick pan, warm the olive oil over medium heat. Vegetables should be sautéed till tender. When the egg mixture is ready, pour it over the vegetables and simmer it. Serve the omelette folded in half.

Dairy-Free Smoothie Bowl

Ingredients:

1 frozen banana

1/2 cup frozen berries (e.g., blueberries, strawberries)

1/2 cup lactose-free yogurt (e.g., almond, coconut, soy-based)

1 tablespoon nut butter (e.g., almond, peanut)

Toppings: sliced fruits, nuts, seeds, and shredded coconut

Instructions:

Blend the frozen banana, frozen berries, lactose-free yogurt, and nut butter until smooth. Pour the smoothie into a bowl and add the toppings your desire.

Chia Seed Pudding

Ingredients:

1/4 cup chia seeds

1 cup lactose-free milk (e.g., almond, oat, soy)

1 tablespoon maple syrup or agave syrup

Fresh fruits for topping

Instructions:

In a bowl, mix chia seeds, lactose-free milk, and sweetener. Stir well and refrigerate overnight or for at least 2 hours. Top with fresh fruits before serving.

Breakfast Burrito

Ingredients:

1 large tortilla (check for lactose-free option)

2 cooked turkey sausages, chopped (check for lactose-free option)

1/4 cup diced tomatoes

1/4 cup diced avocado

2 tablespoons salsa

Fresh cilantro (optional)

Instructions:

Warm the tortilla. Fill it with the cooked turkey sausage, diced tomatoes, diced avocado, salsa, and fresh cilantro (if using). Roll it up and enjoy.

Lactose-Free Pancakes

Ingredients:

1 cup all-purpose flour

1 tablespoon sugar

1 teaspoon baking powder

1/2 teaspoon baking soda

1 cup lactose-free milk (e.g., almond, soy)

1 tablespoon vegetable oil

1 teaspoon vanilla extract

Instructions:

In a bowl, mix the dry ingredients (flour, sugar, baking powder, and baking soda). In a separate bowl, whisk the lactose-free milk, vegetable oil, and vanilla extract. Combine the wet and dry ingredients and stir until just combined. Cook spoonful of batter on a preheated non-stick pan until bubbles form on top, then flip and cook until golden brown.

Dairy-Free Breakfast Muffins

Ingredients:

1 1/2 cups all-purpose flour

1/2 cup sugar

2 teaspoons baking powder

1/2 teaspoon salt

1/2 cup vegetable oil

1/2 cup lactose-free milk (e.g., coconut, almond)

1 teaspoon vanilla extract

1 cup fresh or frozen berries (e.g raspberries)

Instructions:

Heat your oven to 375°F (190°C) and line a muffin tin with liners. In a large bowl, mix the dry ingredients (flour, sugar, baking powder, and salt). In a separate bowl, whisk the vegetable oil, lactose-free milk, and vanilla extract. Add the wet ingredients to the dry ingredients and stir well till combined. Gently fold in the berries. Fill each muffin cup 3/4 full and bake for 18-20 minutes or until a toothpick comes out clean when inserted into the center.

Quinoa Breakfast Bowl

Ingredients:

1 cup cooked quinoa

1/2 cup lactose-free yogurt (e.g., coconut, soy-based)

1 tablespoon honey or maple syrup

Fresh fruits (e.g., berries, mango, kiwi)

1 tablespoon chopped nuts or seeds

Instructions:

In a bowl, mix the cooked quinoa, lactose-free yogurt, and honey/maple syrup. Top with fresh fruits and chopped nuts/seeds.

Dairy-Free Breakfast Burrito Bowl

Ingredients:

1 cup cooked brown rice

1/2 cup black beans (canned, rinsed and drained)

1/4 cup diced avocado

1/4 cup diced tomatoes

2 tablespoons salsa

Fresh cilantro (optional)

Instructions:

In a bowl, layer the cooked brown rice, black beans, diced avocado, diced tomatoes, salsa, and fresh cilantro (if using).

Smashed Chickpea Sandwich

Ingredients:

1 can chickpeas, drained and rinsed

2 tablespoons vegan mayonnaise

1 tablespoon Dijon mustard

1 tablespoon lemon juice

Salt and pepper to taste

Lettuce and sliced tomatoes

2 slices of bread (check for lactose-free option)

Instructions:

Mash the chickpeas with a fork or potato masher in bowl. Stir in the vegan mayonnaise, Dijon mustard, lemon juice, salt, and pepper. Spread the mixture on one slice of bread, top with lettuce and sliced tomatoes, and cover with the other slice of bread.

Dairy-Free Banana Bread

Ingredients:

2 ripe bananas, mashed

1/3 cup vegetable oil

1/2 cup brown sugar

1/4 cup lactose-free milk (e.g., almond, oat)

1 teaspoon vanilla extract

1 1/2 cups all-purpose flour

1 teaspoon baking soda

1/2 teaspoon salt

1/2 teaspoon ground cinnamon (optional)

Instructions:

Heat your oven to 350°F (175°C) and apply grease to a loaf pan. In a large bowl, mix the mashed bananas, vegetable oil, brown sugar, lactose-free milk, and vanilla extract. In a separate bowl, whisk the flour, baking soda, salt, and ground cinnamon (if using). Gradually add the dry ingredients to the wet ingredients and mix properly. Place the greased loaf pan with the batter inside, and bake for 50 to 60 minutes, or until a toothpick inserted in the center comes out clean.

Dairy-Free Breakfast Pizza

Ingredients:

1 pre-made pizza crust (check for lactose-free option)

1/2 cup tomato sauce

1 cup diced veggies (e.g., bell peppers, onions, spinach)

1/4 cup dairy-free cheese (e.g., almond, soy-based)

2-3 sliced cooked turkey sausages (check for lactose-free option)

Fresh basil leaves (optional)

Instructions:

Preheat your oven to the temperature specified on the pizza crust package. Spread the tomato sauce on the pizza crust, leaving a small border around the edges. Top with diced veggies, dairy-free cheese, and sliced turkey sausages.

Bake according to the crust's instructions or until the cheese is melted and bubbly. Garnish with fresh basil leaves if desired.

Dairy-Free Zucchini Fritters

Ingredients:

2 cups grated zucchini (blot up any extra moisture)

1/4 cup chopped green onions

1/4 cup gluten-free flour

2 tablespoons nutritional yeast (for cheesy flavor, optional)

1/2 teaspoon baking powder

Salt and pepper to taste

Olive oil for frying

Instructions:

In a bowl, mix the grated zucchini, green onions, flour, nutritional yeast (if using), baking powder, salt, and pepper. Heat olive oil in a non-stick pan over low heat. Drop spoonful of the zucchini mixture onto the pan and flatten with a spatula. Cook until golden brown on both sides. Serve with dairy-free yogurt or a drizzle of olive oil.

Dairy-Free Blueberry Muffins

Ingredients:

1 1/2 cups all-purpose flour

1/2 cup sugar

1 1/2 teaspoons baking powder

1/4 teaspoon baking soda

1/2 teaspoon salt

1 cup lactose-free milk (e.g., almond, soy-based)

1/4 cup vegetable oil

1 teaspoon vanilla extract

1 cup fresh or frozen blueberries

Instructions:

Heat your oven to 375°F (190°C) and line a muffin tin with liners. In a large bowl, mix the dry ingredients (flour, sugar, baking powder, baking soda, and salt). In a separate bowl, whisk the lactose-free milk, vegetable oil, and vanilla extract. Add the wet ingredients to the dry ingredients and stir properly. Gently fold in the blueberries. Fill each muffin cup 3/4 full and bake for 18-20 minutes or until a toothpick comes out clean when inserted into the center.

LUNCH

Grilled Chicken Salad:

Ingredients:

Grilled Chicken Salad:

1 cup Grilled chicken breast, cooked and chopped

2 cups Mixed greens (lettuce, spinach, arugula)

1 cup Cherry tomatoes, halved

1 cup Cucumbers, sliced

1/4 cup red onions, thinly sliced

2 tablespoons Balsamic vinaigrette dressing

Instructions:

Toss the mixed greens, cherry tomatoes, cucumbers, and red onions in a bowl. Add the grilled chicken on top and drizzle with balsamic vinaigrette dressing.

Quinoa and Roasted Vegetable Bowl:

Ingredients:

1 cup cooked quinoa

1 cup Roasted bell peppers, sliced

1 cup Zucchini, sliced

1 cup Eggplant, diced

1/4 cup red onion, sliced

2 tablespoons Olive oil

2 tablespoons Lemon juice

2 tablespoons Fresh parsley, chopped.

Instructions:

Toss the roasted vegetables with cooked quinoa. Drizzle with olive oil and lemon juice. Top with fresh parsley.

Shrimp Stir-Fry:

Ingredients:

1 cup Shrimp, peeled and deveined

1 cup Broccoli, florets

1/2 cup Carrots, sliced

1/2 cup red bell pepper, sliced

1/2 cup snap peas

2 cloves garlic, minced

1 teaspoon ginger, grated

3 tablespoons soy sauce (check for lactose-free)

1 tablespoon Sesame oil

1 cup cooked rice (optional)

Instructions:

In a wok or large pan, stir-fry the shrimp and vegetables with garlic and ginger. Sesame oil and soy sauce can be used for taste. Serve over cooked rice if desired.

Lentil and Vegetable Soup:

Ingredients:

1 cup red lentils, rinsed

1/2 cup Carrots, diced

1/2 cup Celery, diced

1/2 cup Potatoes, diced

1/2 cup Tomatoes, diced

4 cups Vegetable broth

1 teaspoon Fresh thyme

Salt and pepper, to taste.

Instructions:

In a pot, combine red lentils, chopped vegetables, and vegetable broth. Bring to a boil, then simmer until the lentils and vegetables are tender. Season with salt, fresh thyme, and pepper.

Turkey Avocado Wrap:

Ingredients:

1 cup Sliced turkey breast

1 Avocado, sliced

1 cup Spinach leaves

1/2 cup Sliced red bell pepper

1 Whole-grain wrap or gluten-free wrap.

Instructions:

Lay out the wrap and add the turkey, avocado, spinach, and red bell pepper. Roll it up and slice into smaller pieces.

Tofu and Vegetable Stir-Fry:

Ingredients:

1 block Firm tofu, cubed

1 cup Broccoli, florets

2 cups Bok choy, chopped

1/2 cup red bell pepper, sliced

1/2 cup Snap peas

1 teaspoon Ginger, grated

2 cloves Garlic, minced

3 tablespoons Gluten-free soy sauce

1 tablespoon Sesame oil

1 cup cooked rice or quinoa (optional)

Instructions:

Cube the tofu and stir-fry with chopped vegetables, ginger, and garlic. Boost taste by including gluten free soy sauce and sesame oil. Serve over cooked rice or quinoa if desired.

Mediterranean Chickpea Salad:

Ingredients:

1 can (15 ounces) Canned chickpeas, rinsed and drained

1 cup Cucumber, diced

1 cup Cherry tomatoes, halved

1/4 cup red onion, thinly sliced

1/2 cup Kalamata olives, pitted and halved

2 tablespoons Fresh parsley, chopped

2 tablespoons Lemon juice

2 tablespoons Olive oil

Instructions:

Combine all ingredients in a bowl, then toss with lemon juice and olive oil.

Grilled Salmon with Asparagus:

Ingredients:

2 Salmon fillets

1 bunch Asparagus

2 Lemon wedges

2 tablespoons Olive oil

Salt and pepper, to taste.

Instructions:

Brush the salmon and asparagus with olive oil, season with salt and pepper. Grill until the salmon is cooked through and the asparagus is tender. Serve with lemon wedges.

Chickpea and Avocado Sandwich:

Ingredients:

1 cup Canned chickpeas (mashed)

1 Avocado (mashed)

1/4 cup red onion, diced

2 tablespoons Lemon juice

1 tablespoon Fresh dill, chopped

Salt and pepper, to taste

4 Lettuce leaves.

Instructions:

Spread the mashed chickpeas and avocado on bread slices. Add sliced tomatoes and lettuce. Close the sandwich and cut in half.

Thai Coconut Curry with Vegetables:

Ingredients:

2 cups Mixed vegetables (bell peppers, carrots, zucchini, etc.), chopped

1 can (14 ounces) Coconut milk (check for lactose-free)

2 tablespoons red curry paste (check for lactose-free)

1 teaspoon Ginger, grated

2 cloves Garlic, minced

2 tablespoons Lime juice

2 tablespoons Fresh cilantro, chopped

1 cup cooked rice or rice noodles (optional).

Instructions:

In a pot, combine the mixed vegetables with coconut milk and red curry paste. Add ginger and garlic for flavor. Simmer until the vegetables are cooked through. Add lime juice, then sprinkle fresh cilantro over top. Serve over cooked rice or rice noodles if desired.

Tuna and Avocado Salad:

Ingredients:

1 can (5 ounces) Canned tuna, drained

1 Avocado, diced

1/4 cup red onion, diced

2 tablespoons Lemon juice

1 tablespoon Fresh dill, chopped

Salt and pepper, to taste

4 Lettuce leaves

Instructions:

In a bowl, combine flaked tuna, diced avocado, chopped red onion, and fresh dill. Season with lemon juice, salt, and pepper. Serve with lettuce leaves.

Mexican Black Bean Burrito Bowl:

Ingredients:

1 cup Cooked black beans

1 cup Brown rice, cooked

1 Avocado, sliced

1/2 cup Salsa

1/4 cup Sliced jalapenos

2 tablespoons Fresh cilantro, chopped.

Instructions:

Layer the cooked black beans and brown rice in a bowl. Top with sliced avocado, salsa, sliced jalapenos, and fresh cilantro.

Chicken and Vegetable Kebabs:

Ingredients:

1 pound Chicken breast, cut into cubes

2 cups Bell peppers (various colors), chopped

1/2 cup red onion, chopped

1 cup Zucchini, sliced

2 tablespoons Olive oil

2 tablespoons Lemon juice

1 teaspoon Paprika

Salt and pepper, to taste.

Instructions:

Thread the chicken and vegetables onto skewers. Brush with olive oil and lemon juice, then season with paprika, salt, and pepper. Grill or bake until the chicken is cooked through.

Rice Paper Rolls with Peanut Sauce:

Ingredients:

8 Rice paper wrappers

1 cup Shredded lettuce

1/2 cup Shredded carrots

1/2 cup Cucumber slices

1/4 cup Fresh mint leaves

1 cup cooked rice noodles

Peanut sauce (check for lactose-free) for dipping.

Instructions:

Soak the rice paper wrappers in warm water to soften. Add cooked rice noodles, lettuce, carrots, cucumbers, mint leaves, and lay them out flat. As you roll them up tightly, tuck the sides in. Serve with peanut sauce for dipping.

Vegan Lentil Sloppy Joes:

Ingredients:

2 cups cooked lentils

1/2 cup Diced bell peppers

1/4 cup Chopped onions

1 can (14 ounces) Crushed tomatoes

2 tablespoons Tomato paste

2 tablespoons Brown sugar

2 tablespoons Apple cider vinegar

1 tablespoon Mustard

1 teaspoon Garlic powder

1 teaspoon Chili powder

4 Hamburger buns or gluten-free buns.

Instructions:

In a pan, sauté the diced bell peppers and chopped onions until soft. Add cooked lentils, crushed tomatoes, tomato paste, brown sugar, apple cider vinegar, mustard, garlic powder, and chili powder. Simmer until the mixture thickens. Serve on hamburger buns or gluten-free buns.

DINNER

Grilled Lemon-Herb Chicken:

Ingredients:

4 boneless, skinless chicken breasts

2 tablespoons olive oil

1 tablespoon chopped fresh herbs (rosemary, thyme, or oregano)

Juice and zest of 1 lemon

Salt and pepper to taste

Instructions:

Preheat the grill to medium-high heat.

In a bowl, mix olive oil, lemon juice, zest, chopped herbs, salt, and pepper.

Set aside at least 30 minutes to let the chicken breasts soak up the mixture.

Grill the chicken for about 5-6 minutes per side until fully cooked. Serve with your favorite lactose-free side dishes.

Lactose-Free Beef Stir-Fry:

Ingredients:

1 pound beef strips

2 tablespoons soy sauce (ensure it's lactose-free)

2 tablespoons rice vinegar

1 tablespoon sesame oil

1 tablespoon cornstarch

2 tablespoons vegetable oil

Various stir-fry vegetables, including bell peppers, broccoli, and carrots

Instructions:

In a bowl, combine soy sauce, rice vinegar, sesame oil, and cornstarch to make the marinade.

Add the beef strips to the marinade and let it sit for 15-20 minutes.

Heat the vegetable oil over medium-high heat in a large pan or wok.

Stir-fry the marinated beef until cooked through.

Add the vegetables and cook for an additional 2-3 minutes until tender.

Serve over rice or rice noodles.

Shrimp and Avocado Salad:

Ingredients:

1pound cooked shrimp, peeled and deveined

2 ripe avocados, diced

1 cup cherry tomatoes, halved

1/4 cup chopped cilantro

2 tablespoons lime juice

2 tablespoons olive oil

Salt and pepper to taste

Instructions:

In a large bowl, combine shrimp, diced avocados, cherry tomatoes, and cilantro.

To create the dressing, combine the lime juice, olive oil, salt, and pepper in a separate bowl.

After adding the dressing, carefully toss the salad to incorporate.

Serve as is or with a side of lactose-free tortilla chips.

Quinoa Stuffed Bell Peppers:

Ingredients:

4 large bell peppers (any color)

1 cup cooked quinoa

1 cup black beans (canned and drained)

1 cup diced tomatoes (canned or fresh)

1/2 cup diced red onion

2 cloves garlic, minced

1 teaspoon ground cumin

1 teaspoon chili powder

Salt and pepper to taste

Olive oil for drizzling

Instructions:

Preheat the oven to 375°F (190°C).

Remove the bell peppers' tops, then scoop out the seeds and membranes

In a bowl, mix cooked quinoa, black beans, diced tomatoes, red onion, minced garlic, ground cumin, chili powder, salt, and pepper.

Place the bell peppers in a baking dish after stuffing them with the mixture.

Drizzle olive oil over the stuffed peppers.

Bake for 25-30 minutes or until the peppers are tender and slightly browned on top.

Lactose-Free Chicken Alfredo Pasta:

Ingredients:

1 pound chicken breast, cooked and sliced

12 ounces lactose-free fettuccine pasta

2 tablespoons dairy-free butter

2 cups unsweetened almond milk

2 tablespoons cornstarch

1/2 cup nutritional yeast

2 cloves garlic, minced

Salt and pepper to taste

Fresh parsley for garnish (optional)

Instructions:

Cook the fettuccine pasta according to package instructions.

In a saucepan, melt the dairy-free butter over medium heat.

Add minced garlic and cook until fragrant.

In a small bowl, whisk together almond milk and cornstarch.

Pour the almond milk mixture into the saucepan and stir continuously until the sauce thickens.

Add nutritional yeast, salt, and pepper, and continue stirring until well combined.

Toss the cooked pasta and chicken slices with the lactose-free Alfredo sauce.

Garnish with fresh parsley before serving.

Tofu and Vegetable Curry:

Ingredients:

1 block firm tofu, cubed

1 cup sliced vegetables (zucchini, bell peppers, carrots, etc.)

1 can (14 ounces) coconut milk

2 tablespoons curry powder

1 tablespoon vegetable oil

1 tablespoon soy sauce (lactose-free)

2 cloves garlic, minced

1 tablespoon grated ginger

Cooked rice or quinoa for serving

Instructions:

In a large pan or skillet, heat the vegetable oil over medium heat.

Add the minced garlic and the grated ginger, and cook until fragrant.

Add the cubed tofu and sliced vegetables to the pan and cook for a few minutes until slightly browned.

Stir in the curry powder and soy sauce, mixing well to coat everything.

Pour in the coconut milk, reduce the heat to low, and let it simmer for 10-15 minutes.

Serve the tofu and vegetable curry over cooked rice or quinoa.

Lemon Garlic Roasted Chicken Thighs:

Ingredients:

4 bone-in, skin-on chicken thighs

2 tablespoons olive oil

Juice and zest of 1 lemon

3 cloves garlic, minced

1 teaspoon dried thyme

Salt and pepper to taste

Instructions:

Preheat the oven to 400°F (200°C).

In a bowl, mix olive oil, lemon juice, zest, minced garlic, dried thyme, salt, and pepper.

Place the chicken thighs in a baking dish and pour the lemon-garlic mixture over them, ensuring they are well coated.

Roast in the oven for 25-30 minutes or until the chicken is cooked through and the skin is crispy.

Serve with your favorite lactose-free side dishes.

Grilled Salmon with Mango Salsa:

Ingredients:

4 salmon fillets

1 ripe mango, diced

1/4 cup diced red onion

1/4 cup chopped cilantro

1 jalapeno, seeded and minced

Juice of 1 lime

Salt and pepper to taste

Instructions:

Preheat the grill to medium-high heat.

Season the salmon fillets with salt and pepper.

Grill the salmon for about 4-5 minutes per side until cooked through.

In a bowl, mix diced mango, red onion, cilantro, minced jalapeno, lime juice, salt, and pepper to make the salsa.

Top each grilled salmon fillet with mango salsa before serving.

Lactose-Free Shepherd's Pie:

Ingredients:

1 pound ground beef or lamb

1 cup diced carrots

1 cup frozen peas

1 cup beef or vegetable broth

2 tablespoons tomato paste

1 tablespoon Worcestershire sauce (lactose-free)

1 teaspoon dried thyme

Salt and pepper to taste

4 cups mashed potatoes (made with lactose-free milk and dairy-free butter)

Instructions:

Preheat the oven to 375°F (190°C).

In a large skillet, brown the ground beef or lamb over medium-high heat.

Add diced carrots and frozen peas to the skillet and cook until the vegetables are tender.

Stir in the beef or vegetable broth, tomato paste, Worcestershire sauce, dried thyme, salt, and pepper.

Let the mixture simmer for a few minutes until the sauce thickens.

Transfer the meat and vegetable mixture to a baking dish and spread the mashed potatoes over the top.

The mashed potatoes should be baked in the oven for 20 to 25 minutes, or until golden brown.

Stuffed Zucchini Boats:

Ingredients:

4 medium zucchinis

1 cup cooked quinoa or rice

1 cup diced tomatoes

1 cup cooked ground turkey or chicken

1/2 cup diced bell peppers

2 cloves garlic, minced

1 tablespoon olive oil

1 teaspoon dried oregano

Salt and pepper to taste

Instructions:

Preheat the oven to 375°F (190°C).

Slice each zucchini in half lengthwise and scoop out the flesh, leaving about 1/4inch thick shells.

Garlic cloves should be sautéed in olive oil over medium heat until aromatic.

Add diced tomatoes, cooked ground turkey or chicken, diced bell peppers, dried oregano, salt, and pepper. Cook until heated through.

Stir in the cooked quinoa or rice and mix well.

Stuff the zucchini boats with the filling and place them in a baking dish.

Bake the zucchini for 20 to 25 minutes, or until it is soft.

Lactose-Free Lentil Soup:

Ingredients:

1 cup dried red lentils

1 large onion, diced

2 carrots, diced

2 celery stalks, diced

2 cloves garlic, minced

6 cups vegetable or chicken broth

1 tablespoon olive oil

1 teaspoon ground cumin

1/2 teaspoon ground turmeric

Salt and pepper to taste

Fresh lemon wedges for serving

Instructions:

Heat olive oil over medium heat in a big pot.

Add diced onions, carrots, and celery. Cook until softened.

Stir in minced garlic, ground cumin, ground turmeric, salt, and pepper. Cook for another minute.

Add dried lentils and broth to the pot. Bring to a boil, then reduce heat to low and let it simmer for about 20-25 minutes or until the lentils are tender.

Serve hot with some freshly squeezed lemon juice.

Lactose-Free Veggie Pad Thai:

Ingredients:

8 ounces rice noodles

1 cup sliced tofu or cooked chicken (optional)

1 cup julienned carrots

1 cup bean sprouts

1/2 cup chopped green onions

1/4 cup chopped peanuts

2 tablespoons vegetable oil

3 tablespoons soy sauce (lactose-free)

2 tablespoons tamarind paste

1 tablespoon brown sugar

2 cloves garlic, minced

1 lime, cut into wedges

Instructions:

Prepare the rice noodles according to the package instructions.

In a small bowl, mix soy sauce, tamarind paste, brown sugar, and minced garlic to make the sauce.

Cook for a few minutes until the vegetables are tender-crisp.

If using tofu or chicken, stir-fry until heated through.

Add julienned carrots, bean sprouts, and chopped green onions. Cook the vegetables for a few minutes, or until they are crisp-tender.

Toss in the cooked rice noodles and the sauce, stirring to combine.

Serve with chopped peanuts and lime wedges.

Lactose-Free BBQ Pulled Pork Sandwiches:

Ingredients:

1 pound pork shoulder or pork tenderloin

1 cup lactose-free BBQ sauce

1/2 cup chicken or vegetable broth

1 tablespoon olive oil

Salt and pepper to taste

Hamburger buns (lactose-free or gluten-free)

Instructions:

Season the pork shoulder or tenderloin with salt and pepper.

Heat olive oil over medium-high heat in a large pot.

Brown the pork by pan-searing it on all sides.

Transfer the pork to a slow cooker or instant pot.

Pour in the lactose-free BBQ sauce and chicken or vegetable broth.

Cook on low for 6-8 hours in the slow cooker or follow the manufacturer's instructions for the instant pot.

Use two forks to shred the pork when it has become soft.

Serve the pulled pork on hamburger buns and enjoy your lactose-free BBQ pulled pork sandwiches.

Lactose-Free Lemon Garlic Shrimp Pasta:

Ingredients:

12 ounces gluten-free or lactose-free pasta

1pound large shrimp, peeled and deveined

1/4 cup olive oil

Juice and zest of 1 lemon

4 cloves garlic, minced

1/2 teaspoon crushed red pepper flakes (optional)

Salt and pepper to taste

Fresh parsley for garnish (optional)

Instructions:

As directed on the packaging, cook the pasta.

Olive oil should be heated in a big skillet over a medium heat.

Sauté the minced garlic and red pepper flakes until fragrant.

When the shrimp are pink and opaque, add them to the skillet.

Add the salt, pepper, and lemon juice and zest.

Toss the cooked pasta with the lemon garlic shrimp.

Garnish with fresh parsley before serving.

Lactose-Free Tofu and Vegetable Stir-Fry:

Ingredients:

1 block firm tofu, cubed

2 tablespoons soy sauce (lactose-free)

2 tablespoons rice vinegar

1 tablespoon sesame oil

2 tablespoons cornstarch

2 tablespoons vegetable oil

Assorted stir-fry vegetables (broccoli, bell peppers, snow peas, etc.)

Cooked rice or rice noodles for serving

Instructions:

In a bowl, combine soy sauce, rice vinegar, sesame oil, and cornstarch to make the marinade.

Add the cubed tofu to the marinade and let it sit for 15-20 minutes.

Heat the vegetable oil over medium-high heat in a large pan or wok.

Stir-fry the marinated tofu until lightly browned and crispy.

Add the assorted stir-fry vegetables to the pan and cook for an additional 2-3 minutes until tender.

Serve over cooked rice or rice noodles.

DESSERTS

Lactose-Free Chocolate Brownies

Ingredients:

1 cup all-purpose flour

1 cup granulated sugar

1/2 cup cocoa powder

1/2 cup vegetable oil

1/2 cup lactose-free milk (e.g., almond milk, soy milk)

2 tsp vanilla extract

1 tsp baking powder

Pinch of salt

1/2 cup dairy-free chocolate chips

Instructions:

Preheat your oven to 350°F (175°C) and grease a square baking pan.

Combine the flour, sugar, baking soda, cocoa powder, and salt in a mixing dish.

Add the vegetable oil, lactose-free milk, and vanilla extract. Mix until well combined.

Fold in the dairy-free chocolate chips.

Spread the batter evenly after pouring it into the prepared baking pan.

Bake for 20 to 25 minutes, or until a toothpick inserted in the center emerges with a few moist crumbs.

Allow the brownies cool in the pan before slicing and serving.

Vegan Strawberry Shortcake

Ingredients:

1 cup all-purpose flour

1/4 cup granulated sugar

1 1/2 tsp baking powder

1/4 tsp salt

1/4 cup coconut oil (solid, not melted)

1/2 cup lactose-free milk (e.g., coconut milk, oat milk)

1 tsp vanilla extract

Fresh strawberries, sliced

Dairy-free whipped cream

Instructions:

Set a baking sheet on the bottom of the oven and preheat it to 375°F (190°C).

Combine the flour, sugar, baking soda, and salt in a mixing basin.

Once the mixture resembles coarse crumbs, add the coconut oil using a pastry cutter or fork.

Add the lactose-free milk and vanilla extract. Mix until a dough forms.

Drop spoonfuls of dough onto the prepared baking sheet to form shortcakes.

Bake for 15-18 minutes or until the shortcakes are golden brown.

Let them cool slightly before assembling with sliced strawberries and dairy-free whipped cream.

Dairy-Free Mango Sorbet

Ingredients:

3 cups frozen mango chunks

1/4 cup maple syrup or agave nectar

1/4 cup water

1 tbsp lime juice

Instructions:

In a blender or food processor, combine frozen mango chunks, maple syrup, water, and lime juice.

Blend until it's creamy and smooth, stopping to scrape the sides as necessary.

Transfer the mixture to a shallow container and freeze for at least 4 hours or until firm.

Serve the mango sorbet in scoops and enjoy.

Lactose-Free Lemon Bars

Ingredients:

1 cup all-purpose flour

1/2 cup powdered sugar

1/2 cup dairy-free margarine

2 tbsp cornstarch

1 cup granulated sugar

1/4 cup lemon juice

Zest of one lemon

1/4 cup lactose-free milk (e.g., rice milk, cashew milk)

Instructions:

Preheat your oven to 350°F (175°C) and grease a square baking pan.

In a mixing bowl, combine the flour and powdered sugar.

Cut in the dairy-free margarine until the mixture resembles coarse crumbs.

Bake for 15 minutes after pressing the mixture into the prepared baking pan.

Meanwhile, whisk together cornstarch, granulated sugar, lemon juice, lemon zest, and lactose-free milk until smooth.

The half-baked crust should be covered with the lemon mixture.

Once the filling is set, bake for another 20 to 25 minutes.

Let the lemon bars to cool completely before cutting into squares.

Dairy-Free Chocolate Mousse

Ingredients:

1 can (14 oz) full-fat coconut milk, refrigerated overnight

1/4 cup cocoa powder

1/4 cup powdered sugar

1 tsp vanilla extract

Instructions:

Open the chilled coconut milk and scoop the thick, creamy part into a mixing bowl, leaving the watery part behind.

Using a hand mixer or stand mixer, whip the coconut cream until fluffy.

Add cocoa powder, powdered sugar, and vanilla extract. Whip again until well combined.

Transfer the chocolate mousse to serving glasses or bowls and refrigerate for at least 1 hour before serving.

Vegan Banana Bread

Ingredients:

1 1/2 cups mashed ripe bananas (about 5 bananas)

1/3 cup vegetable oil

1/2 cup granulated sugar

1/4 cup lactose-free milk (e.g., almond milk, hemp milk)

1 tsp vanilla extract

1 3/4 cups all-purpose flour

1 tsp baking soda

1/2 tsp salt

Instructions:

Grease a loaf pan and set the oven to 350°F (175°C).

In a mixing bowl, combine mashed bananas, vegetable oil, sugar, lactose-free milk, and vanilla extract.

Mix the flour, salt, and baking soda in another basin.

Add the dry ingredients in small amounts to the wet ones and whisk just until incorporated.

After smoothing the top, pour the batter into the prepared loaf pan.

Allow to bake for 50-60 minutes or until a toothpick inserted in the center comes out clean.

Let the banana bread to cool in the pan for 10 minutes before transferring it to a wire rack to cool completely.

Lactose-Free Rice Pudding

Ingredients:

1 cup cooked white rice

2 cups lactose-free milk (e.g., soy milk, coconut milk)

1/4 cup granulated sugar

1/4 tsp salt

1 tsp vanilla extract

Ground cinnamon for garnish

Instructions:

In a saucepan, combine cooked rice, lactose-free milk, sugar, and salt.

Over medium heat, whisk the mixture often as it simmers.

Reduce the heat to low and let it simmer for 20-25 minutes, stirring occasionally, until the mixture thickens to a creamy consistency.

Vanilla extract should be added after the pan has been taken off the heat.

Serve the rice pudding warm or chilled, garnished with ground cinnamon.

Dairy-Free Apple Crisp

Ingredients:

4 cups sliced apples (any variety)

1/2 cup granulated sugar

1 tbsp lemon juice

1/2 tsp ground cinnamon

1/4 tsp ground nutmeg

1/2 cup rolled oats

1/4 cup all-purpose flour

1/4 cup brown sugar

1/4 cup dairy-free margarine, melted

Instructions:

Preheat your oven to 350°F (175°C) and grease a baking dish.

In a large bowl, toss the sliced apples with granulated sugar, lemon juice, cinnamon, and nutmeg.

Place the prepared baking dish with the apple mixture inside.

In a separate bowl, combine rolled oats, all-purpose flour, brown sugar, and melted dairy-free margarine.

Evenly cover the apples with the oat mixture.

Bake for 30-35 minutes, or until the apples are soft and the topping is golden brown.

Let the apple crisp cool slightly before serving. Enjoy it as is or with a scoop of lactose-free ice cream.

Vegan Coconut Macaroons

Ingredients:

2 cups shredded coconut

1/2 cup granulated sugar

1/4 cup aquafaba (liquid from a can of chickpeas)

1 tsp vanilla extract

Pinch of salt

Dairy-free chocolate chips (optional)

Instructions:

Set a baking sheet on your oven's 350°F (175°C) rack and preheat the oven.

In a mixing bowl, combine shredded coconut, granulated sugar, aquafaba, vanilla extract, and salt.

Mix the ingredients thoroughly with your hands.

Scoop tablespoon-sized portions of the mixture onto the prepared baking sheet, shaping them into macaroons.

If desired, press a few dairy-free chocolate chips onto the top of each macaroon.

Bake the macaroons for 15 to 18 minutes, or until they are slightly brown.

Allow them to cool on the baking sheet before serving.

Dairy-Free Cherry Almond Crumble

Ingredients:

4 cups pitted cherries (fresh or frozen)

1/4 cup granulated sugar

1 tbsp cornstarch

1 tsp almond extract

1 cup rolled oats

1/2 cup all-purpose flour

1/2 cup sliced almonds

1/4 cup coconut oil, melted

1/4 cup maple syrup

Instructions:

Grease a baking dish and preheat the oven to 375°F (190°C).

In a large bowl, toss the pitted cherries with granulated sugar, cornstarch, and almond extract.

Transfer the cherry mixture to the prepared baking dish.

In a separate bowl, combine rolled oats, all-purpose flour, sliced almonds, melted coconut oil, and maple syrup.

Crumble the oat mixture over the cherries in the baking dish.

Bake for 30-35 minutes or until the crumble topping is golden and the cherries are bubbling.

Let the cherry almond crumble cool slightly before serving.

Vegan Chocolate Avocado Pudding

Ingredients:

2 ripe avocados

1/4 cup cocoa powder

1/4 cup maple syrup or agave nectar

1/4 cup lactose-free milk (e.g., almond milk, soy milk)

1 tsp vanilla extract

Pinch of salt

Dairy-free chocolate chips for garnish (optional)

Instructions:

Cut the avocados in half, remove the pits, and scoop the flesh into a blender or food processor.

Add cocoa powder, maple syrup, lactose-free milk, vanilla extract, and salt to the blender.

Blend the ingredients until they are creamy and smooth, scraping down the sides as necessary.

Transfer the chocolate avocado pudding to serving cups or bowls.

If desired, sprinkle dairy-free chocolate chips on top for garnish.

Refrigerate the pudding for at least 30 minutes before serving.

Lactose-Free Peanut Butter Cookies

Ingredients:

1 cup creamy peanut butter

1 cup granulated sugar

1 tsp baking powder

1/4 cup lactose-free milk (e.g., almond milk, coconut milk)

1 tsp vanilla extract

Instructions:

Set a baking sheet on your oven's 350°F (175°C) rack and preheat the oven.

In a mixing bowl, combine peanut butter, granulated sugar, baking powder, lactose-free milk, and vanilla extract.

Mix until a smooth dough forms.

Create little balls out of the dough and set them on the baking sheet that has been prepared.

Use a fork to make a crisscross pattern on each cookie, flattening them slightly.

Bake for 10 to 12 minutes, or until the edges are just beginning to turn brown.

The cookies should cool for a short while on the baking sheet before being moved to a wire rack to finish cooling.

Dairy-Free Raspberry Chia Seed Pudding

Ingredients:

1 cup lactose-free milk (e.g., almond milk, rice milk)

1/4 cup chia seeds

2 tbsp maple syrup or agave nectar

1 tsp vanilla extract

Fresh raspberries for garnish

Instructions:

In a jar or airtight container, combine lactose-free milk, chia seeds, maple syrup, and vanilla extract.

Stir thoroughly to distribute the chia seeds evenly.

Seal the container and refrigerate for at least 4 hours or preferably overnight.

Stir the chia seed pudding thoroughly before serving.

Top with fresh raspberries before serving.

Vegan Oatmeal Raisin Cookies

Ingredients:

1 cup rolled oats

1 cup all-purpose flour

1/2 cup coconut oil, melted

1/2 cup granulated sugar

1/4 cup lactose-free milk (e.g., oat milk, almond milk)

1 tsp vanilla extract

1 tsp ground cinnamon

1/2 tsp baking soda

1/4 tsp salt

1/2 cup raisins

Instructions:

Set a baking sheet on your oven's 350°F (175°C) rack and preheat the oven.

In a mixing bowl, combine rolled oats, all-purpose flour, melted coconut oil, granulated sugar, lactose-free milk, vanilla extract, ground cinnamon, baking soda, and salt.

Mix until a dough forms.

Fold in the raisins.

Drop spoonfuls of dough onto the prepared baking sheet, spacing them apart.

Flatten each cookie slightly with your fingers.

Bake the cookies for 10 to 12 minutes, or until they are just brown.

The cookies should cool for a few minutes on the baking sheet before being moved to a wire rack to finish cooling.

Dairy-Free Coconut Ice Cream

Ingredients:

2 cans (28 oz) full-fat coconut milk, refrigerated overnight

1/2 cup granulated sugar

1 tsp vanilla extract

1 cup shredded coconut (toasted, optional)

Instructions:

Open the chilled coconut milk and scoop the thick, creamy part into a mixing bowl, leaving the watery part behind.

Using a hand mixer or stand mixer, whip the coconut cream until fluffy.

Add granulated sugar and vanilla extract. Whip again until well combined.

If desired, stir in toasted shredded coconut for extra texture and flavor.

Transfer the coconut ice cream mixture to a shallow container and freeze for at least 4 hours or until firm.

Serve the coconut ice cream in scoops and enjoy.

CONCLUSION

In conclusion, lactose intolerance is a common digestive disorder that occurs due to the body's inability to fully digest lactose, the sugar found in milk and dairy products. While it can cause discomfort and inconvenience, individuals with lactose intolerance can still enjoy a variety of meals that promote both nutritional balance and digestive well-being.

The key to managing lactose intolerance lies in making thoughtful dietary choices. Incorporating lactose-free or low-lactose alternatives, such as lactose-free milk and dairy products, can help individuals maintain their calcium and nutrient intake without triggering symptoms. Additionally, the inclusion of fermented dairy products like yogurt and kefir can often be better tolerated due to their naturally reduced lactose content and beneficial probiotics that aid digestion.

Choosing meals rich in non-dairy sources of calcium, such as leafy greens, fortified plant-based milks, and fortified orange juice, can help ensure that individuals with lactose intolerance still meet their nutritional needs. Furthermore, embracing a diet rich in whole, unprocessed foods including lean proteins, whole grains, fruits, and vegetables can help alleviate digestive discomfort and promote overall well-being.

By being attentive to one's body and its responses, individuals can identify their personal lactose tolerance levels and tailor their meals accordingly. This might involve consuming smaller portions of lactose-containing foods, spacing them throughout the day, or opting for lactase enzyme supplements when enjoying dairy-rich meals.

In essence, while lactose intolerance may require dietary adjustments, it does not mean sacrificing taste, variety, or nutritional value. With the right choices, individuals can create meals that nourish their bodies and support digestive comfort, allowing them to fully enjoy a well-rounded and satisfying diet.

Made in United States
Troutdale, OR
12/06/2023

15453399R00046